Who Was
Frida Kahlo?

Who Was
Frida Kahlo?

by Sarah Fabiny

illustrated by Jerry Hoare

Penguin Workshop

To Phyllis and Bob, thank you for everything—SF

For Lynne—JH

PENGUIN WORKSHOP
An Imprint of Penguin Random House LLC, New York

If you purchased this book without a cover, you should be aware that this book is stolen property. It was reported as "unsold and destroyed" to the publisher, and neither the author nor the publisher has received any payment for this "stripped book."

Visit us online at www.penguinrandomhouse.com.

Library of Congress Control Number: 2013032704

ISBN 9780448479385   30 29 28 27

Contents

Who Was Frida Kahlo?..1

Little Frida..4

A Show of Spirit...13

An Artist Is Born...25

Meeting Diego Again...37

Life in the United States.......................................47

Ups and Downs..62

Up and Up..71

Painting through the Pain.....................................80

Undying Spirit...89

Timelines..102

Bibliography...105

Where to Find Frida Kahlo's Paintings............106

Who Was
Frida Kahlo?

Viva la vida! In English that means "Long live life!" Frida Kahlo put these words into one of the last paintings she did. They were words that Frida kept in her head and in her heart throughout her life.

When she was only eighteen years old, Frida was involved in a terrible bus accident. Her injuries were very bad, and at first no one knew if she would survive. Frida had to stay in bed for months. Many of her bones were broken, and she was in a lot of pain. But Frida was a strong and stubborn person, and she was determined to get better.

At the time of the accident, Frida had been studying to become a doctor. She was smart and curious and loved school, but her injuries meant she was no longer able to go to classes. Bored by having to lie in bed while she recuperated, Frida asked her father if she could borrow his paints and

paintbrushes. Frida created many paintings while she recovered. She soon realized that she didn't want to be a doctor—she wanted to be an artist.

The accident that caused Frida pain and suffering throughout her life also inspired her. By painting, Frida was able to get through the difficult times. She was a strong and courageous person who was determined never to stop telling the world *Viva la vida!*

Chapter 1
Little Frida

Magdalena Carmen Frida Kahlo y Calderón was born on July 6, 1907, in Coyoacán, Mexico. Her father was Guillermo Kahlo. He had immigrated to Mexico from Germany in 1891. Her mother was Matilde Calderón y Gonzalez. She was Mexican, and her family was descended from American Indian and Spanish blood.

Frida was born at La Casa Azul (the Blue House), a house her father had built for his family in 1904. It was called the Blue House because the outside was painted a bright blue. The house would become an important part of Frida's life.

Frida's father had several jobs after he moved to Mexico. But when he married Frida's mother, she talked him into becoming a photographer, which was what her own father had been. As it turned out, Guillermo Kahlo was a very good photographer and was very successful. The

Mexican government asked Mr. Kahlo to take photographs of the landscapes and historical buildings of Mexico. For about four years he traveled all over Mexico and took hundreds of photographs. Frida grew up looking at her father's photographs. They helped her learn about Mexican history, art, and architecture.

But Frida wasn't just curious to learn about

 the history, art, and architecture of the country she was born in. She also wanted to learn about nature and science. Frida was always bringing home rocks, insects, plants, and even small animals. Frida's mother wasn't always happy to have bugs and frogs in the house, but her father thought this was fantastic. He wanted his daughter to learn as much as she could.

Frida had three sisters—Matilde and Adriana, who were older, and Cristina, who was younger. But Frida was definitely her father's favorite. He thought Frida was the smartest and the most like him.

Frida's father liked to paint when he wasn't busy taking photographs. He sometimes took Frida with him when he traveled to the countryside to paint. Frida would watch her father use his paints and brushes.

When Frida was six years old, she caught a serious disease called polio. Polio is a disease that affects the brain and spine, and it sometimes leaves people paralyzed. Frida survived polio, but it took a long time for her to get better. She had to stay in her room at the Blue House for almost nine months. It was hard for someone as curious and energetic as Frida to be stuck in bed. But Frida made up an imaginary friend to keep her company when she was alone.

Because of the polio, Frida's right leg became weak and thin. But her parents didn't want her to stop doing things because of her leg. She played soccer, wrestled, boxed, and was a champion swimmer. These were all things that girls didn't usually do in Mexico in the early 1900s.

Even with all the exercise, Frida's leg did not grow stronger. The kids in her neighborhood and at school teased her about her leg. They called her *pata de palo*, which means "peg leg." Frida would yell back at them. She was determined not to let the nickname or her weak leg stop her.

As she got older, Frida wore pants, long dresses, and skirts to hide her leg. She also wore three or four pairs of socks and a special shoe. Frida didn't want anyone to know she was different, make fun of her, or feel sorry for her.

Chapter 2
A Show of Spirit

Even though Frida had missed a lot of school because of her illness, she was a good student and got good grades. Frida had a photographic memory, which meant she could picture something in her head after she had seen or read it. It was also easy for Frida to learn languages, and she was able to read and speak Spanish, English, and German. It was clear to Frida's parents that their daughter was very bright and loved to learn.

Because of that, they agreed to let her attend the Escuela Nacional Preparatoria (National Preparatory School) in Mexico City. It was the best high school in the country. So when she was fifteen years old, Frida and thirty-four other girls

joined a school with two thousand boys. But Frida wasn't afraid or worried. She knew she was smart, and she knew that she would do well.

Frida was away from home for the first time. It opened her eyes, her head, and her heart to lots of new things. The big, bustling capital city had been at the heart of the Mexican Revolution, which had lasted from 1910 to 1920. The friends Frida made, the things they talked about, and what she was learning in class all changed Frida's life. She was no longer Frida Peg Leg. Her classmates saw her as a smart, fun, mischievous girl who could do anything she put her mind to.

Frida took all kinds of classes in high school. Her favorite subjects were science and math. Although Frida's father and grandfather had been photographers, Frida decided she wanted to be a doctor.

That was unusual for a young girl in Mexico at that time. It would not be easy and would take many years, but Frida was determined to do it.

Even though Frida and her friends studied hard, they also liked to have fun—especially Frida. She joined a group called the Cachuchas. This was the name of the special red caps they all wore. The group was made up of seven boys and two girls. The leader of the group was Alejandro Gómez Arias. He became Frida's boyfriend.

Frida loved hanging out with her friends. More than anything, they liked to play pranks and practical jokes on people. Frida was popular in the group because she was so daring and brave. She didn't care if she got into trouble. She liked being a troublemaker and annoying her teachers.

After the revolution, one of the first things the new Mexican government did was to hire artists to paint large scenes on the walls of

buildings for everyone to see. These paintings,
called murals, showed the history of Mexico.
The new government wanted to help Mexicans

understand their past, make them proud of their
country, and give them hope for a better future.

HISTORY OF MEXICO

ANCIENT CIVILIZATIONS SUCH AS THE TOLTECS, THE MAYANS, AND THE AZTECS LIVED IN MEXICO FOR THOUSANDS OF YEARS. THEY BUILT TOWERING TEMPLES WHERE THEY WORSHIPED THEIR POWERFUL GODS AND PRAYED TO THE SUN AND MOON. THEY CREATED AMAZING ARTWORK, JEWELRY, POTTERY, AND TEXTILES.

THIS ALL CHANGED WHEN THE SPANISH ARRIVED IN MEXICO IN 1519. THEY BROUGHT THEIR LANGUAGE, THEIR WAY OF LIFE, AND THEIR STYLE OF EUROPEAN ART AND ARCHITECTURE WITH THEM. THE NATIVE PEOPLE OF MEXICO AND THE SPANISH FOUGHT FOR MANY YEARS, BUT THE SPANISH ULTIMATELY CONQUERED AND COLONIZED MEXICO. THEN IN 1810, MEXICO DECLARED ITS INDEPENDENCE FROM SPAIN. THE NEW COUNTRY AND ITS CITIZENS WERE A MIX OF ALL THESE CULTURES.

One day, an artist named Diego Rivera came to Frida's school. Diego Rivera was very famous for his murals, and it was an honor for the school to have him there. Frida didn't care that he was famous. She liked calling him "old fatso" while he was trying to work. Frida also did things like stealing food from his lunch box and putting soap on the stairs to see if he would slip and fall.

Frida got into so much trouble that she was expelled from school. But Frida felt that this was unfair, and she decided to do something about it. She took her case straight to the minister of public education. What an incredibly

brave thing to do! The minister agreed to let Frida go back to school. But that didn't change her behavior. She went back to school and continued to do silly and crazy things.

The years at high school changed Frida, and it made her more determined to stay strong and accomplish whatever she wanted. She was on her way to becoming a doctor. Frida felt that she had so much to live for. But all of that would soon change.

Chapter 3
An Artist Is Born

Every day after school Frida would take the bus home from Mexico City to the Blue House in Coyoacán. On September 17, 1925, Frida and Alejandro got on the bus and found seats together at the back. As the bus slowed down to make a turn, it was hit by a streetcar. The bus was crushed. Alejandro was thrown out of the bus and under the streetcar. Frida was trapped inside. The metal arm from one of the bus seats had gone through Frida's body.

Alejandro watched as a passerby pulled the piece of metal out of Frida's body. After a few minutes an ambulance arrived and took Frida to the hospital.

The doctors took Frida to the operating room. Her injuries were so bad that they weren't sure if she would survive. Frida's spinal column and many bones in her body had been broken. Frida's family was so upset by what had happened that they didn't want to see her in the hospital. Her sister Matilde was the only person in the 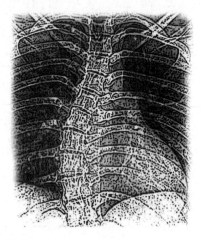 family who visited. Matilde visited Frida every day while she lay in the hospital in a full-body plaster cast. Matilde made Frida laugh and helped her take her mind off her injuries.

The Cachuchas also visited Frida in the hospital.
She was happy to have friends who reminded her of
all the fun and enjoyment of school.

But when Matilde and her friends left at night,
Frida was all alone. She thought a lot about how
she might have died in the accident. The memories
of that horrible day stayed with Frida for her
whole life. But she was a strong person. She had
overcome polio, and she was determined that

the accident would not stop her, either.

After a month in the hospital, the doctors told Frida she was strong enough to go home. But Frida's bones did not heal properly, and she was in constant pain for the rest of her life.

Frida was still in her full-body plaster cast. She couldn't move or sit up in bed. To help recover from polio, Frida had done all kinds of sports.

Now she just had to lie still. The usually daring, mischievous girl needed something to do.

Frida asked her father if she could borrow his paints. She had never thought about being an artist, but she had often gone with her father when he painted. Frida's mother had a carpenter make a special easel so that Frida could paint while she was lying on her back in bed. Frida also

had a big mirror put up over her bed so that she could look at herself while she painted. "I paint myself because I am so often alone," Frida said, "and because I am the subject I know best."

Although she eventually was able to walk again, for the next two years Frida went back and forth to the hospital for more operations. She spent a lot of time lying on her back in bed. And going back to school was out of the question. But Frida still managed to paint. She had found something she really loved doing.

Frida painted the things that were familiar and that she knew best—her friends and family and herself. She got ideas on how to paint by reading her father's art books. She copied the paintings displayed in these books. But Frida also wanted her paintings to show the things she loved about her own country. She thought about the history that mural artists like Diego Rivera showed in their work. Frida started to include religious symbols

and images from Mexican folk art in her paintings. She felt that all these things reflected who she was and what was important to her.

Frida was determined never to let her accident and the pain stop her from enjoying life. She started seeing her friends and going to parties—

and she kept on painting. Painting made her forget the pain and feel well enough to start doing things again.

In the two years after her accident, Frida painted over twenty-four pictures.

THE MEXICAN REVOLUTION,
1910–1920

WHEN MEXICO GAINED INDEPENDENCE FROM SPAIN IN 1821, IT WAS A POOR COUNTRY. MOST MEXICANS WORKED ON FARMS ALL DAY LONG FOR VERY LITTLE PAY. GOVERNMENT OFFICIALS AND A FEW RICH FARM OWNERS KEPT THE MONEY FOR THEMSELVES. IN 1910, THE MEXICAN PEOPLE ROSE UP AGAINST THE GOVERNMENT. THEY HAD HAD ENOUGH AND WANTED THE COUNTRY TO CHANGE.

EMILIANO ZAPATA AND PANCHO VILLA

WITH LEADERS LIKE EMILIANO ZAPATA AND
PANCHO VILLA, THE REVOLUTION HELPED PUT
A NEW GOVERNMENT IN PLACE. THE NEW
GOVERNMENT PROMISED TO MAKE LIFE FAIR
FOR EVERYONE IN MEXICO.

Frida did not really show her paintings to many people. She was mainly painting for herself and to help herself feel better. And from the very beginning, Frida had a special way of painting.

Chapter 4
Meeting Diego Again

Frida loved meeting up with her friends and going to parties with them. She and her friends talked about politics and art and literature.

It helped her forget the sad things that had happened to her. Diego Rivera was at one of the parties Frida went to. He did not remember Frida, but she remembered him.

A few days after that party, Frida had an idea. She decided to take four of her paintings and show them to Diego. Frida thought he would be able to tell her whether she was any good at painting. Although she had made fun of him years before, Frida still respected his talent. Diego was painting one of his murals and was up on a tall scaffolding. "Diego, come down! I have something important to discuss with you!" Frida called up to him. He probably thought that was a very brave and bold thing for Frida to do.

Diego looked at the paintings that Frida had brought. He said that three of them were too influenced by other paintings Frida had seen. But he really liked one of the paintings. It was a self-portrait—a painting that Frida had done of herself "It's original," Diego said. "You have talent." He knew that Frida could be a painter.

Diego told Frida to go home and paint another portrait. He said that he would come to her house the following Sunday to look at it. Diego kept his word and went to see Frida's painting. Frida showed him all the paintings she had done so far. Although she was only twenty-one years old at the time, Diego was impressed with Frida's work and her talent. He was also impressed by her energy.

Diego started to spend a lot of time with Frida at the Blue House. Eventually he started to fall in love with her, and Frida started to fall in love with Diego.

Even though Diego was almost twice Frida's age, her father saw that the couple loved each other and was happy for them to be together. Mr. Kahlo knew that Diego would be a good teacher for Frida. He called them "the elephant and the dove" because Diego was so big  and round, and Frida was small and delicate.

 Mr. Kahlo warned Diego that his daughter could be mischievous and a troublemaker, but Diego didn't care.

Part of the reason Diego loved Frida was because she was so unique. She wove ribbons and flowers into her hair. She wore lots of jewelry and traditional Mexican costumes. Diego also liked that she reflected Mexican culture in her paintings and in the way she looked.

DIEGO RIVERA

DIEGO RIVERA WON A SCHOLARSHIP TO STUDY ART IN EUROPE WHEN HE WAS TWENTY. HE LIVED IN PARIS FOR MANY YEARS AND LEARNED TO PAINT

LIKE EUROPEAN ARTISTS. DIEGO RETURNED TO MEXICO IN 1921, JUST AFTER THE MEXICAN REVOLUTION. HE DECIDED THAT HE WANTED TO PAINT THINGS THAT SHOWED THE HISTORY OF MEXICO AND ITS PEOPLE. HE TURNED AWAY FROM THE STYLES HE HAD STUDIED WHILE IN EUROPE, AND HE PAINTED BIG, BRIGHT, BOLD MURALS THAT WERE NOT LIKE ANYTHING HE HAD PAINTED BEFORE.

DIEGO BELIEVED THAT ART WASN'T JUST FOR RICH PEOPLE, AND THAT EVERYONE SHOULD HAVE A CHANCE TO SEE PAINTINGS. SO DIEGO'S MURALS SHOWED ORDINARY PEOPLE—FARMERS, MINERS, AND FACTORY WORKERS. HIS MURALS REFLECTED THE THINGS THE MEXICAN REVOLUTION HAD BEEN FOUGHT FOR.

Frida and Diego were married in 1929. Some of Frida's friends were surprised that she decided to marry someone so much older than she. But that didn't matter to Frida. He was Mexico's greatest artist, and Frida knew she could learn a lot from him.

Chapter 5
Life in the United States

Frida did not paint much after she and Diego were married. Looking after her husband was a full-time job. He sometimes worked for eighteen hours a day, seven days a week. Frida would go and sit with Diego while he painted. She even learned to cook the foods that Diego liked to eat. Frida was frustrated that she wasn't painting,

but she didn't say anything to Diego. She felt it was her responsibility to look after her famous husband. How would the world get to see Diego's incredible murals if she wasn't helping behind the scenes?

The year after Frida and Diego were married, Diego was asked to work in the United States. In November 1930, the couple traveled to San Francisco. Because Diego was so famous, Frida

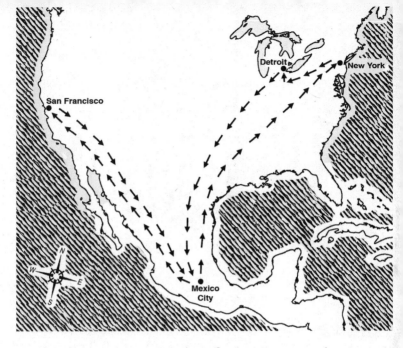

and Diego were invited to fancy parties when they arrived. The "elephant and dove" were very popular with the high society in San Francisco.

But once Diego started working on his mural, Frida ended up spending a lot of time on her own. She did not feel comfortable in the United States, and she missed Mexico. It was also the time of the Great Depression in the United States. Even though Frida and her husband met a lot of

wealthy people while they were in San Francisco, Frida saw a lot of poor people when she took walks around the city.

Frida and Diego were fun to be around, and people liked spending time with them—they told funny jokes and interesting stories, and they laughed a lot. However, things didn't always go well between the two of them. They were both strong and stubborn, and they argued. Frida felt she and Diego were spending too much time in the United States. She was homesick and wanted to go back to Mexico.

Frida didn't really make friends with anyone while she was in San Francisco. But one person she met there became a big part of her life. His name was Dr. Leo Eloesser. He became her friend and her doctor. For the rest of her life, he treated Frida whenever she was sick or in pain.

During this time, Frida painted *Frieda and Diego Rivera*. The picture shows the couple on their wedding day. In the painting Diego is much bigger than Frida. He holds a painter's palette and brushes. This was Frida's way of showing that she admired him as an artist. She is dressed

DR. LEO ELOESSER

in traditional Mexican clothing and jewelry and has leaves in her hair. Above her is a dove. Maybe Frida was thinking of how her father called the couple "the elephant and the dove."

Diego and Frida went back to Mexico for a short time in 1931. Diego needed to finish a painting that he had started there. While they were in Mexico, they stayed in the Blue House. Diego liked Frida's family home, but he decided to build a new house for them in San Angel. It would really be two buildings connected with a bridge. Frida would live in one part of the house, and Diego would live and work in the other part of the house.

Frida was happy to be back home, but she soon had to pack her suitcases and leave again. The Museum of Modern Art in New York City wanted to present an exhibition of Diego's work. Frida did not really want to go back to the United States, but it was a very big honor for her husband.

FRIDA AND DIEGO'S HOME IN SAN ANGEL.

While she was in New York, Frida again met lots of rich and famous people. But just like in San Francisco, there were many people in New York City who were unemployed and hungry due to the Depression. It made Frida sad. She was upset that she and Diego were having a good time and going to fantastic parties while many people were suffering.

After Diego's exhibition closed, he and Frida moved to Detroit. The Ford Motor Company had asked Diego to paint a mural for them. While Diego was busy painting, so was Frida. She decided to paint how she felt about being away from home and how she didn't always like being in the United States.

In 1932, Frida painted a picture called *Self-Portrait on the Borderline between Mexico and the United States*. Frida is in the middle of the painting. On one side of her are ancient Mexican ruins. Around the ruins are beautiful flowers and big, bright vegetables. On the other side of Frida are tall skyscrapers and smokestacks puffing out pollution into the sky. Through the painting Frida was letting people know how she much she loved

and missed her homeland, and that she didn't care for the fast-paced industrialized world outside it.

Another painting Frida did a year later is called *My Dress Hangs Here*. In the painting you can tell that being in New York City didn't always make Frida happy. It shows many people standing in line waiting for food, a building on fire, and an overflowing garbage can. Frida even included a toilet in the painting. But she didn't put herself in the picture. Instead, she painted one of her dresses hanging from a line in the middle of the scene. Frida's message is that while her dress may be in New York City, her body and soul are in Mexico.

THE GREAT DEPRESSION

IN OCTOBER 1929, THE STOCK MARKET IN THE UNITED STATES CRASHED. THE INVESTMENTS THAT THOUSANDS OF PEOPLE HAD MADE IN THE STOCK MARKET WERE WIPED OUT. BANKS, FACTORIES, AND STORES CLOSED. MILLIONS OF AMERICANS LOST THEIR JOBS AND THEIR SAVINGS. THIS CRASH LED TO THE GREAT DEPRESSION. DURING THIS TIME, LIFE WAS VERY DIFFICULT, AND MANY PEOPLE CAME TO DEPEND ON THE GOVERNMENT OR CHARITY TO PROVIDE THEM WITH FOOD AND HOUSING.

Chapter 6
Ups and Downs

After three years in the United States, Frida and Diego moved back to the house that Diego had built for them in Mexico. As planned, Frida

lived in one side of the house, which was painted blue just like the Blue House, and Diego lived in the other. They had been arguing more and more while they were in the United States. Living in separate wings of the house made life and work easier for both of them.

Arguing with Diego upset Frida, but she put her emotion and energy into her paintings. It was during these difficult times that Frida sometimes painted her best and most interesting pictures.

While they were in the United States, Diego had been getting most of the attention. However, Frida felt it was now her turn to show the world that she was also a talented artist.

Frida did some of her paintings on metal or wood rather than on canvas. Painting on metal or wood was popular in Mexican folk art. Choosing to follow this style of painting was a way for Frida to express the importance of her culture and country in her artwork.

During this time Frida had to have even more operations. She also found out that she would never be able to have a baby. Frida wanted to have children, but her injuries from the accident meant she would never be able to. This sad news was one more thing that Frida had to bear. Life just seemed so unfair. Some of the things that Frida painted are difficult to understand and quite hard to look at. But she always told the story of her own life in her paintings, and she was not afraid

to express her feelings through her art. Frida often included images of Mexican history and filled them with symbols from Mexican art and culture. She wanted to remind people of her pride in her country.

At one point Frida and Diego had such a big argument that Frida moved out of the house in San Angel. She cut off all her long, beautiful hair and stopped wearing the traditional Mexican clothes she had always worn. It was the exact opposite of how Frida really was, and it showed how upset she was by what had happened between her and Diego.

Even though Frida's personal life was difficult, she was becoming more successful as an artist. People were beginning to pay more attention to her paintings. They were fascinated by the way she showed her feelings and her thoughts in her pictures. She was becoming as famous as her husband.

Frida did a painting in 1937 called *Memory*, or *The Heart*. In it, Frida appears without her hands, to show that she is helpless. She seems to float in the air. A large heart lies on the ground. There is a hole where her heart should be, and a sword has been pushed through the hole. Frida used

parts of her body to symbolize how heartbroken and powerless she was to change things between herself and Diego. In some ways, putting these images into her art helped Frida feel better about the things she could not control.

Later in 1937, Frida's paintings were included in a group exhibit at the National Autonomous

University of Mexico. Julian Levy, the owner of a gallery in New York City, was at the exhibit. He thought Frida's paintings were fascinating. When he got back to New York, he wrote to Frida. He asked her if she would show her paintings at his gallery. It was just the break that Frida had been waiting for. Frida replied, "Yes!" and sent

photos of some of her other paintings. Mr. Levy asked Frida if she could send thirty paintings for the exhibition. So Frida got to work and started painting more than ever.

Chapter 7
Up and Up

Frida worked for the next year to finish the new paintings for her exhibition in New York City. In October 1938, she traveled to New York for her first solo show. It was an exciting time for Frida.

She had wanted to be thought of as an artist in her own right. But she was also scared. She was worried that people might not like her work. But Diego encouraged her to go. He knew that Frida was ready for this. He also knew that the world was ready for her style of artwork.

At the exhibition opening, Frida looked amazing. She wore traditional Mexican clothing and jewelry, and bright ribbons in her hair. It was almost as if Frida was a work of art herself!

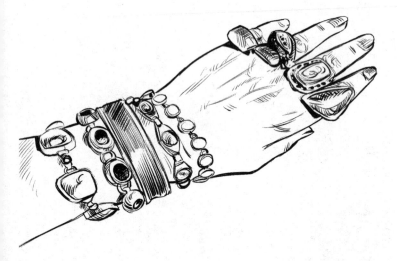

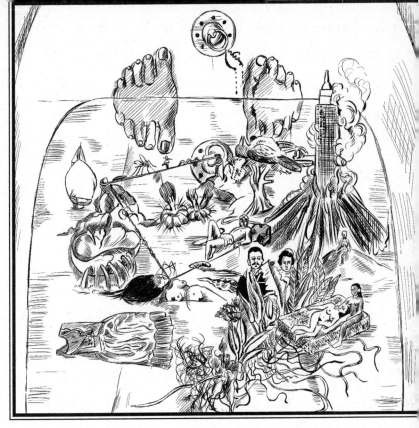

One of the paintings that Frida did for her exhibit was called *What the Water Gave Me*. It shows Frida's lower legs and feet as she sits in a bathtub. There are all kinds of objects floating in the water that represent both happy and sad moments from Frida's life. The painting is like a dream in some ways. It was a way for Frida to look at all the events that had happened to her in her life. Perhaps it was what Frida actually thought about when she sat in her bathtub.

Other painters at the time were painting in a similar way. Their style was called surrealism. Surrealist painters didn't try to show what things looked like in the real world. They tried to portray dreams or even nightmares. They wanted to express the unconscious mind.

An art critic who saw *What the Water Gave Me* called Frida a surrealist. It is easy to see why some people thought Frida was a surrealist: Her paintings often included strange things. But Frida never wanted her style of painting to be given a label. She said, "I never painted dreams. I painted my own reality."

The opening of Frida's show was a big and exciting moment for the art world in New York City. Many famous people were invited to come.

They had never really seen anything like the
paintings that Frida had created. Some people
didn't know what to think about Frida's work and
criticized it. But most people praised not only her
paintings but also Frida herself. They liked her
strong spirit, her colorful way of dressing, and her

unique style. Frida felt that she had finally been recognized as a true artist. Half of the paintings in the exhibit were sold, and some people even asked Frida to paint pictures for them.

While she was in New York City, Frida loved to sit in cafés and watch people walk by. She just wanted to soak up the city and not paint or sketch. She also loved exploring the different neighborhoods in the city. And wherever she went, she caused a sensation because she was always dressed in her Mexican costumes. Frida liked the attention. She felt that people were interested in her because of who she was, not because she was Diego Rivera's wife.

A NEW WAY OF PAINTING

SURREALISM IS AN ART MOVEMENT THAT WAS STARTED IN EUROPE IN THE 1920S. SURREALIST ARTISTS WANTED TO FREE PEOPLE FROM AN "ORDINARY" WAY OF THINKING. THEIR PICTURES OFTEN ATTEMPT TO SHOW THE MYSTERIOUS WORLD OF PEOPLE'S DREAMS. SURREALISTS DIDN'T WANT THEIR WORK TO MAKE SIMPLE, LOGICAL SENSE. THIS IS WHY MANY OF THE PAINTINGS LOOK LIKE SCENES FROM A DREAM OR A NIGHTMARE.

SALVADOR DALÍ

TWO OF THE MOST FAMOUS SURREALIST ARTISTS WERE SALVADOR DALÍ (1904-1989) AND MAX ERNST (1891-1976). THEIR PAINTINGS WERE FILLED WITH FAMILIAR OBJECTS THAT WERE PAINTED TO LOOK STRANGE OR MYSTERIOUS. SURREALISTS HOPED THEIR ODD PAINTINGS WOULD MAKE PEOPLE LOOK AT THINGS IN A NEW AND DIFFERENT WAY, AND CHANGE THE WAY THEY FELT ABOUT ART AND LIFE.

MAX ERNST

Chapter 8
Painting through the Pain

News of Frida's success in New York City spread. She was asked to exhibit some of her work in Paris, France. So in January 1939, Frida got on a boat and sailed to Paris. She was alone on this trip because Diego was ill and couldn't travel. But Frida was more confident about going on her own this time. Her trip to New York had proven that people respected her and her work. She didn't need Diego to help her deal with people, the art world, or a big city.

Seventeen of Frida's paintings were included in an exhibition called *Mexique*. The exhibition included her work as well as photographs of Mexico, pre-Columbian sculpture (sculpture created before Columbus sailed to the New

World), and Mexican folk art. Frida was happy that her paintings were being shown with other things from her country. It was a good way for people in Paris to learn about Mexico—and also about Frida.

One of Frida's paintings in the exhibit was called *The Frame*. It was a self-portrait showing Frida with flowers and ribbons in her hair. Frida had painted it on aluminum, but the frame was painted on glass that was placed on top of the metal. On the frame are bright flowers and two birds.

The prestigious Louvre Museum in Paris bought the painting. It was the first painting by a twentieth-century Mexican artist to be purchased by this world-famous museum. Frida could hardly believe it.

While she was in Paris, Frida met some famous artists who lived in the city, including Pablo Picasso. He was one of the most well-known artists in the world, and his paintings helped create what we now think of as "modern art." Picasso

PABLO PICASSO

was impressed by Frida's talent and by her style.

He liked that Frida dressed in native Mexican costumes and did not care about fitting in with the fashions of the day. Picasso gave Frida a pair of earrings as a gift.

The earrings were in the shape of hands. Frida wore them in a self-portrait she painted two years later. Picasso also taught Frida a Spanish song called "El Huérfano." It became a favorite of hers, and she continued to sing it for the rest of her life.

Even though the Paris art world loved her, Frida was ready to go back to Mexico. But when Frida got back to the house in San Angel, she and Diego argued more than ever. Frida loved her husband, but Diego had been sick for the past three years and hadn't done much of his own painting while he was ill. Perhaps he was angry with Frida because she was becoming so successful. Frida decided that the only way she could still work and stay friends with Diego was to move into her parents' home, the Blue House. Finally, at the end of 1939, Frida and Diego decided to get a divorce.

Frida created some of her best work during this

time, including a painting called *Las Dos Fridas* (The Two Fridas). It shows two Fridas sitting next to each other and holding hands. One Frida is in a stylish white dress. The other is in a traditional Mexican costume. Both Fridas have their hearts on the outsides of their bodies. It isn't an easy painting to look at, but it was Frida's way of showing how upset she was about the divorce and not being with Diego.

Most of the paintings that Frida did during this period were self-portraits. In these paintings, Frida looks straight out, always very serious. Some of them show just Frida's head and shoulders. Others are filled with symbols that reveal what Frida was feeling and thinking.

SELF-PORTRAITS

OF THE ALMOST 150 PAINTINGS THAT FRIDA CREATED, OVER HALF OF THEM WERE SELF-PORTRAITS. FRIDA SAID SHE PAINTED HERSELF MORE THAN ANY OTHER SUBJECT BECAUSE SHE KNEW HERSELF SO WELL. SHE NEVER SMILED IN HER SELF-PORTRAITS. (IT IS SAID THIS IS BECAUSE SHE HAD BAD TEETH.) HER SERIOUS FACE GIVES THE PAINTINGS A CERTAIN SOLEMN FEELING. IT IS PERHAPS A MESSAGE FROM FRIDA THAT ALTHOUGH SHE LOVED HAVING FUN AND ENJOYING HERSELF, MUCH OF HER LIFE HAD BEEN SPENT IN PAIN AND OVERCOMING HARDSHIP.

Chapter 9
Undying Spirit

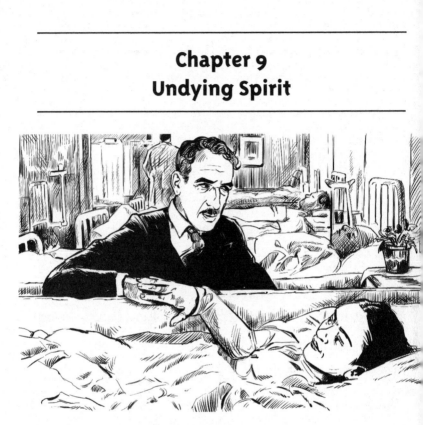

In early 1940, Frida's reputation as a painter started to really take off. Her work was shown at exhibitions in San Francisco and New York. In September of that year, Frida traveled to San Francisco for her show, but also to see Dr. Eloesser.

A doctor in Mexico had told Frida she needed more surgery. Frida wanted Dr. Eloesser to give her a second opinion. Dr. Eloesser told Frida she didn't need surgery, but he checked her into the hospital for rest.

By coincidence, Diego was also in San Francisco at that time. Dr. Eloesser convinced him to go see Frida while she was in the hospital. Frida and Diego truly missed each other, and they missed the support they gave each other in their work. Frida and Diego decided to get married again and to live together in the Blue House. Frida would paint there, and Diego would use the house in San Angel as his studio. They repainted the Blue House a special blue (*azul anil* in Spanish). The color was meant to keep away evil spirits, and Frida and Diego were hoping for a fresh start in their life together.

Frida continued to create amazing and curious paintings. She did many simple self-portraits that

showed her with the parrots and monkeys she kept as pets. But she also did some more complex and symbolic paintings such as *Without Hope* and *The Little Deer*. Frida wasn't afraid to reveal her innermost thoughts and feelings in her paintings. And the world was getting used to seeing artwork like this.

In 1943, Frida was asked to teach at the School of Painting and Sculpture. It had only recently been opened, and it was an honor for Frida to join the staff. Frida taught a painting class twelve times a week. Frida must have really loved teaching and her students (who became known as Los Fridos) to teach that many classes.

Frida also became a member of the Seminario de Cultura Mexicana. This was a group of artists and writers who promoted Mexican art and culture. It was the perfect opportunity for Frida to introduce Mexico, Mexican art, and Mexican culture to people around the world.

As time passed, Frida started having more and more health issues. Most of the problems had been caused by the bus accident years ago. She had many operations on her back and her right leg. Frida was in a lot of pain and once again had to spend lots of time resting in bed. To help her deal with the pain and boredom this time, she started keeping a diary. Frida always found a way to get through the tough times in life.

In the late 1940s, Frida was still painting constantly. While she had done many self-portraits in the past, Frida was now painting still lifes—paintings of arranged objects. Since it was getting hard for Frida to move around, it was easier for her to paint things that could be placed in front of her and that didn't move. But Frida was still able to express her thoughts and feelings in the still lifes. Some of the fruit that Frida painted was shown as damaged and bruised. Some people think this was her way of showing her damaged and bruised body.

Although Frida had had solo exhibits in other countries, there had never been a solo show of her work in Mexico. Finally, in April 1953, Frida had her first solo exhibit in Mexico. Frida's doctor told her that she was too sick to go to the opening. But Frida didn't listen to him. Her bed was put on a truck and set up in the center of the gallery. Frida

was taken to the gallery in an ambulance. When she got there, she was carried to the bed on a stretcher. It seemed as if Frida was a piece of art in her own exhibition.

Frida was a very strong-willed woman, but her body was getting weaker. On July 13, 1954, Frida died at the Blue House—the very place she had been born forty-seven years earlier.

WORLD-FAMOUS

DURING HER LIFE, FRIDA KAHLO'S FAME WAS LIMITED. SHE WAS KNOWN IN MEXICO AND IN SEVERAL BIG CITIES WHERE HER PAINTINGS HAD BEEN SHOWN. IN 1958, THE BLUE HOUSE WAS OPENED AS A MUSEUM. PEOPLE COULD SEE THE STUDIO WHERE FRIDA PAINTED, THE BED SHE SLEPT IN, AND HER COLLECTION OF MEXICAN ART. WORD OF FRIDA'S AMAZING HOUSE AND LIFE AND WORK SPREAD. PEOPLE WANTED TO KNOW MORE ABOUT THIS INCREDIBLE WOMAN. HER DIARY WAS TRANSLATED INTO MANY LANGUAGES, AND THERE WAS EVEN A MOVIE MADE ABOUT HER LIFE. MANY PEOPLE FEEL THAT FRIDA'S SUFFERING AND ART SYMBOLIZED MEXICO'S STRUGGLE TO FIND ITS OWN IDENTITY AS A COUNTRY.

TIMELINE OF FRIDA KAHLO'S LIFE

1907 —— July 6, Magdalena Carmen Frida Kahlo y Calderón born in Coyoacán, Mexico (although she claimed to have been born in 1910, the year the Mexican Revolution started)

1913 —— Contracts polio

1922 —— Enrolls in the National Preparatory School in Mexico City and meets Diego Rivera

1925 —— Severely injured in a bus accident

1926 —— Paints *Self-Portrait in a Velvet Dress*, first serious work

1928 —— Meets Rivera again and shows him some of her paintings

1929 —— Marries Rivera

1930 —— Moves to the United States with Rivera

1933 —— Returns to Mexico with Rivera

1938 —— First solo exhibition, New York City

1939 —— Divorces Rivera; Louvre buys *The Frame*

1940 —— Remarries Rivera

1941 —— Father dies

1943 —— Becomes a teacher at the School of Painting and Sculpture

1946 —— Awarded the National Prize of Arts and Sciences

1953 —— First solo exhibition in her native Mexico

1954 —— Dies July 13, at the age of forty-seven

TIMELINE OF
THE WORLD

Mexican Revolution starts	1910
Marcel Duchamp paints *Nude Descending a Staircase, No. 2*	1912
World War I starts	1914
World War I ends	1918
Mexican Revolution ends	1920
Max Ernst paints *Ubu Imperator*	1923
The US stock market crashes, setting off the Great Depression	1929
Construction begins on the Empire State Building	1930
Salvador Dalí paints *The Persistence of Memory*	1931
Spanish Civil War starts	1936
Pablo Picasso paints *Guernica*	1937
World War II begins Spanish Civil War ends	1939
Leon Trotsky assassinated	1940
World War II ends	1945
Joseph Stalin, the leader of the Soviet Union, dies	1953

BIBLIOGRAPHY

*Frith, Margaret. **Frida Kahlo: The Artist Who Painted Herself.** New York: Grosset & Dunlap, 2003.

Herrera, Hayden. **Frida: A Biography of Frida Kahlo.** New York: Harper & Row, 1983.

*Holzhey, Magdalena. **Frida Kahlo: The Artist in the Blue House.** New York: Prestel Publishing, 2003.

*Laidlaw, Jill A. **Frida Kahlo.** New York: Franklin Watts, 2003.

*Schümann, Bettina. **13 Women Artists Children Should Know.** New York: Prestel Publishing, 2009.

*Venezia, Mike. **Frida Kahlo.** Danbury, CT: Children's Press, 1999.

* Books for young readers

Where to Find Frida Kahlo's Paintings

Albright-Knox Art Gallery, Buffalo, New York

Madison Museum of Contemporary Art, Madison, Wisconsin

Museo Frida Kahlo, Mexico City, Mexico

Museum of Modern Art, New York, New York

National Gallery of Art, Washington, DC

National Museum of Women in the Arts, Washington, DC

San Francisco Museum of Modern Art, San Francisco, California